"Tyagini ji, can't believe I'm thanking you"

Bizarre

Indian Housewife

Gunjan Panjwani

Invincible Publishers

First Printing: 2019

ISBN: 978-93-89600-01-8

Invincible Publishers

Registered Address: 201A, SAS Tower, Sector 38,
Gurgaon - 122003

Acknowledgement

Thank you is just a small word to say to all those who stood along with me in this entertaining journey of getting my work published. I feel extreme gratitude for my source of inspiration, my mentor, my teacher, Dimpy Saini ma'am who guided me to stand for myself and taught me to never look back, as the roads I crossed to make this happen were soiled with dream crushers. I feel indebted to you ma'am to make me believe in myself and become independent. Thank you for making me realise that I have a team of undergirds.

A heartfelt thanks to my mother who was there through all my goods and bads.

Deepa Purswani Chawla, thank you from the bottom of my heart. You always boosted me and chose to review my poems unbiased.

A warm thanks to my editor, Chandni Mathur with whose suggestions I brought forth a delicacy of my uncooked visions.

Also, I want to thank all those who were not there to support me because it's because of them that I came to know how far I could go and how much potential I have.

Preface

Housewife is an underrated term in small towns and big ones alike. But yes, this agenda still prevails; being a housewife is one of the biggest challenges, the highest unpaid job in this world but still seen or estimated as ordinary. If you see carefully the passions of those ladies who had to quit their ambitions in order to serve and live for the family, you'll find a legend in every corner of every house, in every street. Yet they are the real heroes behind the story of each family, be it bringing up children, looking after the husband or other members, they simply are there all the time for you and demand nothing in return but love and respect.

One of the biggest failures in your life is not having the courage to say what you feel or need. I have always been a victim of this syndrome. While reading this, many of you would identify yourself with this kind of behaviour.

This book is all about my experiences as a poetess. It was what I always wanted to be. I was weak, so my words were my strength in most of the poems. You'll find situations from which housewives evolve; challenges of the daily rut. And then in-between you meet some interesting people and you choose to open up to them. I had a meeting with one such sweet person and it all started with writing my first poem in just a span of 20 minutes—raw but specific. The rest just followed.

In this book you will mostly find and see situations expressed directly through the heart of a housewife who lives in a joint but very weirdly entertaining family with thumping gossips and other bizarrely interesting day to day happenings but how I managed to happily survive because of my support of my shenanigans and how it expounded in my little diary, makes my story.

Table of Contents

I miss my maid
perks of toiletries

My maid had an off today
And so was my mood after hearing this
My mind started doing mathematical analysis
Should I go for a headache or knee pain?
I know ultimately this all is gonna go in vain

So it all started with tying my hair into a bun
It was me and dirty house one on one
My broom and I gazed at each other
It said I'll give you a hand don't bother

Both my kids were crying
My phone's battery was dying
I had to swab the floor
Breakfast time appeared
My daughter will miss the bus I feared
Dusting was pending to the core

My maid might be having hiccups all day
Perks of toiletries were on their halfway
"Honey where are my shoes?"
While searching for them I got a bruise

Can't it be the other way round,
Where responsibilities are not bound?
Living a maid's life is not easy
They adore their work
They have their own swag and quirk
Unlike them, we are somewhat similar
Facing those challenges with smiles
Go get up lady you have the strength to go miles

Reigns of rains

The clouds are roaring
convulse I feel
Thirsty is my body
This very moment I wanna steal

The first drop touched me
Made me blush from the core
Marshmallows were my cheeks
and thunders to explore

The drops that you drop
Are a physical blessing
Showers that you shower upon
are like cream cheese dressing

Let's sign a contract
that you'll never go.
And I promise that I will
make this world an ecstatic flow

Here I claim
that rains are my only pure love
Likings are secondary
Billions of kisses
you give me without any boundary

Every organ of mine
for you is the same
People who give excuses
to get wet are just lame

The sound of you roaring
is like music to my ears
When I dance onto your Joy
I let go of all my fears
PS: Dear rains, will you marry me

Momos

Hand in hand commitments withstand
Honeymoon, love, himalayan street
MOMOS
Evening munchies demanding crunchies
Called up the buddies to come out “let’s go”
MOMOS
Hiked and tired taste buds desired
Mouth watered glancing at the red sauce
MOMOS
Shopping done, energy is dun
Footpath and bags loaded but wait
MOMOS
Casual client meeting; sun is over heating
Soft drinks, and what more?
MOMOS
Break up with the boyfriend
Surroundings in a mood to contend
How do I cheer myself up?
MOMOS

What are momos

North eastern delicacies and a treat to us

Don’t you dare call them dimsums or dumplings

They are simply MOMOS

The first night

When I see into your eyes I can hear the silences within you
When I see your face I can read the gestures and that's true
When I see your body I know that you are all mine, my paradise in hue
Cogent is our affinity
No promises but till infinity
You can be my best friend,
my buddy, my fiancé,
my wife, my mistress
or simply just be what you are,
as our love is ageless
Where my imagination stops
Your poise starts
The thought of 🤔💭even parting our ways
Shakes my limbs
As we both are our cupid's victims
what's beyond I cannot see
what's beneath I cannot seek

in-between there is a line
Who wants to go inside?
more and more, do nothing else
but just explore...explore and more...

Windows of memories

I wish a wish that I wish I could go back to my yore.

To my first school, and those studently matters and their core.

The sweet noise of Cuckoo bird

The enchantment of dew drops in foggy mornings

Those exam fears and childish blithers

To that every mistake that I made and being punished

To those group penalties that we paid during not bringing the homework copies

That different sharing

That stupid caring

The first day after vacations

The last day of examinations

The illusions outside classrooms

Those sweepers and their brooms

Sudden news of teachers meeting
After that every student gets busy greeting

That warm heat during winter mornings
Those pinching words of teacher's warnings
That heavenly feeling of being selected as a monitor
We feel as if we are the only creator

That blah-blah laughs we had during boring periods
That staring of teachers after getting caught by them and sudden silence
That blaming each other and getting violent
The selection of students for competitions
The feeling of envy when not selected but still enjoying without any complications

That teasing each other in assembly
That feeling low when uniform is not properly ironed

Creating fake tears and becoming dramatically stressed

That canteen craze during recess

Eating loads of junk food; spoiling school dress

Creating a mess

The passing by of big boys staring and smiling

Those first crushes and hidden feelings

Those healthy encounters with the ones you like

And when finding them in a crowd

Your heart giving a miss

That craving to bunk to avoid the math teacher

Saying in our hearts "what an irritating creature!! "

That involvement in stupid matters but being valued now

This all had to become a past anyhow

We may have become rich now
We may be settled
We may be highly educated
But one thing that can never be calculated
And that's the measurement of
THE WINDOWS OF MEMORIES

Take away my money
But give me back those days

Early marriage

An excitement raised and I got married,
Rendering about family future-got worried
It's nice to start a relation faithfully
The response sure comes to you honestly
But...somewhere it is proved wrong because of bad timing
The flower had still not blossomed and it was plucked out
Someone was to get angry; someone was to shout
The acceptance was not even ready for acceptation
Only the biggest thing was exception

Saying the history repeats itself is a fact
Making my sustenance cornered was a good tact
Is it a rule not ever to dethrone your post?
Is it a rule you always remain the host?
Somewhere I was a victim who said "yes"

Somewhere God was always there to "bless"
Come what may I was not ready
But responsibilities were waiting at the family junction
My nature changed, my attitude changed (I regret)
Finally became that rotten apple without any assumption

Risen from all of them however
But because of that phase
I'll be ignored forever

In-between came a rainbow
A sad rainbow
A wonderful bliss from tip to toe
Always sleeping, always angry with life
but still wanting to give it a second chance
A time for cheerfulness
a time for heavenly dance

I unlocked her emotions, broke her laws
Made her happy, tired up her jaws
Stupidity, stupidity and always stupidity was done
She was the one for me and I was for her the one
I always made her excited
she always made me calm
We walked through the sands of glee, palm in palm

Time went on, this relation became strong
A brand freak + one simply a freak
A spoilt brat + a box of chitchat
One crazy for friends + a girl with only a few friends
A pampered one + an always avoided one

Made of fantastic combination
Everybody started talking about us, feeling friction

But still our hearts were bound with conviction
Ups and downs were a part of this junction

But that was all set apart
Then came a twist and everyone smiled
Finally, the door got knocked
That was good really, but gave us a shock
A bright future, of fulfillment of desires; a good destiny
A bag full of wishes coming true
As if Santa's fixed them forever with a glue
Everything is perfect, everything is fine
We both will remain for each other like a pair of old wine
I think a person changes a bit
But I honestly only want a bit

It's all vision after all
If I see it's all jungle
If I see there is always madness around

But the time is now for you to open up yourself
Occupy with him your romantic shelf
Good deeds have given rewards
and your preparation for that has remained
This moment cannot ever be explained
An excitement has been raised and you'll get married
please ever don't get worried

You will remain a princess, and you were since you were born
No matter what, life will always go on

Words in solitude

What can you define in solitude?
Is it the heart that is empty?
Or the feelings that are suppressed?
Words unexpressed

The hurts are counted as infinity
reputation blindly following gravity
Not all the time can one glee
Though there are reasons
But they are not too prominent
If chicane is everything
Then faith will always remain feared

It's not that we have to listen
To all that that flows through the air
The art of intelligence is a nightmare
And even the true heart is worthless
Why there is a rule of partiality
The one who follows everything
Still loses her dignity

(At the end, everything will be alright. If it doesn't that means it's not the end)
All this proved wrong
If there are countless sad endings
Countless untruly endings
Then where will love land
When it makes a new beginning
hand in hand?

Why the weak is always suppressed?
With the soul so stressed?
Doing is part of karma
God always punishes for wrongs
But if, good deeds are always a result of bad punishment
Then the self-respect and confidence ruins, and grows with a bad nourishment

What is the fault of a basic nature
If not learnt something

There is always a power inside to do everything

13 to 19, an age of many phases of life

but not commitments, loneliness, sadness

20-25 an age of manifesting an encyclopedia of different natures, feelings, persons but not to become an amateur mother.

Why the personal life is not ruled by our self-kingdom?

Why are our words, expression still without freedom?

You have to get humiliated whether as wives or mothers

Our own self is planned by others

Even with a reason

you are not allowed

to make your own decision

Why is that always show-off is counted
Be quiet otherwise the situation will get haunted
Gaining sympathy always for something that is history
I think this family will always remain a mystery

Motherhood

I got pregnant in my thoughts
And told you, you're the father
Your chauvinism climbed up high
And spoke proudly
As if you had won a prize
I am the man
What did you do?

I bleed every month
To get this project through
Thought broke, I balanced and stepped aside
I didn't say yes to you and saved my pride.

I got pregnant in my thoughts
This time I was prepared
You were the one more cherished than
Me
Held my hand and said
We'll do this together no matter what odds we face

I will never let you disgrace
Two faces of a thought coin
One betrayal and other trust purloin...

Midnight and me!!

Modified schemes

Every second to bring you back or compromise

But instead I decided to have

Swollen eyes

Cried out loud last night

I had these visions claiming you mine

Offering me the higher dimensions of new perspectives everyday

But rays of defeat too were walking along my way

What remained constant was that my spine was erect and unafraid was my esteem now

This path is full of thorns

And far away there's a wall to cross

But the road is stuffed with flings, unnecessary emotions, morasses

Courage is ruptured but hope is alive, hale and hearty

After I cross the wall there is something that I'll gain

But is unknown since the character

assassination will still remain
What awaits me is my success
But destiny demands a heavy price in excess
PS
Do I really deserve what makes me truly happy?

I am not snow White

Seven dwarfs of snow white
She was lucky to have got them
Who protected her, pampered her
With what she wanted, whatever she not
She was fortunate to have them all
But I am more fluky than them after all
May be not dwarfs
May be not seven
Nine are they and a feeling of heaven
I fly, I float, I desire with them
I dance, I enjoy, I get along
Far away from the actual realities of life
I remain with them in a zone which is rife
Ignoring the futuristic bitter relations of husband and wife
Like the king who gave an apple to snow white
and she fell in love with him
I don't even need that to make it happen
But of course, pizzas, burgers, noodles and no gym

They fill my time with stupid special effects
But I like those, this is a fact
Till they exist, they are friends, they are mine
Not seven but they are naughty nine.

As if I don't know

As if I don't know
What depth can be raised by enviousness

The joys are separated from a hearty center
It's really a complicated but common one
Bitching, biting, keeping against
Away even from LOC

Only plant remained, which inside was a tree
Good thoughts, misconceptions, worldly happiness
Likings blown up in the air like smoke for free

Is it ok to imitate someone?
Feathering, featuring up different personalities
According to the mood the action will react
Not the original but people will enact

The galaxy of cleverness but at a margin of cleanliness
Making the mindset according to the mind of the owner

Being a leader coming from the lower corner
How can fear in the eyes of elders remains like a Banyan tree
Is it not allowed to open up yourself for free?

Rudeness is also very small
Not a single true feeling out of all

A character-a door again and again opened and closed
When opened its something else,
when closed its something else

The pleasant thinking gone away just after the big occasion

Not even sparing the blood relations
How much can a heart, a mind bear?
Where the chances of hopes are rare
Pessimistic vibrations coming from everywhere

They never in life can go
Tell me about it
As if I don't know

Feelings! I think

When people got angry there was something I lost

Why does it hurt when you love someone the most?

Coming all the way from grievances, returning back again to them

Something went a little wrong

You're gone away from someone you closely belong

Once in a while you can sacrifice the world for just a smile

And that converted into drops of saline fluid in just a while

It's common, but a rare case for us

Caring ,sharing ,stupidity for us

Love ,comments, unreal jealousy for us

These all are a part of true bonding I think.

But this is not bonding, these are feelings! I think!

Relations

Wonders of deep thought, imaginations
Sometimes fulfilling promises, sometimes breaking relations

Like the deep ray of the sun
And the first sight of the moon

The pleasant feeling
Now being broken up into pieces

It usually happens when someone gets high life
It usually happens when someone gets a beautiful wife
It usually happens when mind works like a sharp knife

When jealousy converts into ego
No one's there to help us in our troubles
When trials become failures

Then tears flow like bubbles
Our sympathy becomes fake
Just like a bitter chocolate cake

It usually happens when a relationship fails
It usually happens when joint houses feel like jails
It usually happens when it's difficult to get bail
No word for relations when broken up into pieces
The bad world then delves into thesis
We don't have a choice
But of course, we can raise our voice

A bet in dept

Fortunes at stake
Friendships proselyted fake
Cricket deals speculated
Lost, mind frowned and frustrated
A bet in debt

College freshers opposite about to graduate
Suppressed to articulate
Rising ragging diverted to depression
Mental compression
A bet in debt

Biting nails in tension
Gaining your crush's attention
Failures in love affairs
From hope to despairs
1000 bucks she's mine
Lost and paid, fine
A bet in debt

Whiskey and two glasses
Playing cards; festive season
Common story of masses
Home, street corner, rotten beer bars
Fights provoked; relations poked
Everything finished with permanent scars
A bet in debt

Monsoons in forest

Clear skies sorcerers were the birds
Amazed trees were absolutely nerds

Peacocks were ecstatic
As the wet soil was aromatic

Forest was praising holidays
Monsoon was celebrating birthdays

Joyous was the existence
Apoplectic sun was in long distance

Even the fallen flowers were blooming
The whole existence was booming

Animals were reserved in their elite actions
Nothing in this monsoon was in fractions

As if the time should halt or slow down
Frogs and their so called dictatorship crown

Everything was in absolute harmony
Whether zoology or botany

Eyes behind the spectacles

I saw a human cumin today
Popping up in the butter of life
Her eyes behind the spectacles
Green and XL lashes

Seductive voice with
Vibgyor character reflections
Innocent heart with dusky complexions
As she climbed up the stairs of the stage
She was scared

But her spirit was coruscating
With the joy of being alive
And speaking about the struggles
She faced
The negations she handled

She was forced to depart
From her passions

She smiled
She was forced to quit her desires
She waited

Backstabbed, got up
Criticized, still patient
Believed, got heighted
Belied, got highlighted

Please don't stop believing
Start working with dedication...

Bow down

Bow down to the trees
That witnessed you passing by
Bow down to the streets
On which you walked bare foot
Because they touched them

Bow down to the reflections of energies around you
Because you can count on them
To grow to glow to flow
With sedulous poise

Bow down to the magical moments
That create miracles easily
Bow down to the entities
disguised as your guardian angels
Which construct a cocoon to bolster you

Bowing is becoming ardent
Towards the gifts you receive
Every day to keep you moving
Auras that struggle to paste smiles
Not on the face but eyes as well

Bow down to the mountains
That are still throughout and on...
As they are in deep meditations

Raise your frequencies of gratitude
As this process forms a healthy magnitude

The 90's poem

Once upon a walkman
Pencils were rolled up in the cassettes to get back in
Shakti man
Was our superhero
Frisbees were our souls
Bouncing in joy from here to there
Those days digital and smart was the enthusiasm

Once upon a playground
Sun was the charger
No PUBG it was hide-n-seek
No Instagram but genuine likes and followers of each other

We saw sailing ourselves with paper boats in rainwater
The restless yet lively
The yen to go out and play

Wet mud, sand, pebbles and clay
Once upon a street
There were bets of marbles
Striking which one was stressed upon
Scooby-Doo had the power to scare us
Experiments in Dexter's lab were taken literally...
Our second home Cartoon Network...

Once upon a childhood, we left this all behind
With the growth of technology
I wanna go rewind

Enchantresses

You are the soul between the length of my aspirations
We the boundless we the unbind
We the demonic filth
We the enchantresses
This brace to each other
This grace to each other
Is what keeps us together
We the sufferers of external knowledge and wisdom
We do not know the extent of the importance to each other
But as a leaf is thirsty for rains
So are we I guess

We the mortal entity
In lust to become one
One with THE one
Am I writing this consciously? Maybe no
Apart from the lies

Of the world yes this is true
Still I do not know
Of that which is beyond right and wrong
Of that which is beyond ups and downs
Of that which is beyond all the logics
Of that which is beyond purity and impurity!
Is our end
The end that creates a new beginning
The hope for the present, dancing
Dancing in the waves of joy
With the celebrations of solitude
Rising up on a new attitude!

Today, tomorrow or life ahead
This happiness should be widespread
Happy be the soul
Happy be the goal!

You cannot resist the fact that
The now is us!
The now cannot be hidden
The suffering will break us to the bliss
A bliss of the inner core!

Fake figments?

I see my wings fly up high in the sky
I see my glorious smile never fading away
I see my mother's lap and womb at the same time
I see me moving from I want to I am
I see myself from compulsive to conscious

I see this never closing cage
I see Shiva and Shakti
I see monsoons inside my body
I see eternal bliss embody
I see oceans inside my eyes
Oceans of joy and beatitude
I see gratitude pouring out of my body
I see harmony around me
I do not see the rain, I am the rain
I see emancipation
I see strength
Strength of *sanjeevani*

I see visions, clear visions
I see *nishchalatattvam*
I see energies bouncing up high

I see the signs of the ultimate
I see the Science behind the boundaries
I see my spirit strive
I see bondages disappearing
I see courage manifesting
I see the creator inside me
I see the creation inside me

I see paradise beneath my feet
I see heavens down to me, to greet
I see praises of poor to the almighty
I see the hymns sung by the needy
I see the paths
Paths of the sages who travelled
Travelled with dignity

I see my master
Holding my hands
Tight, never to let go
I see dances of joy and clarity
I see me laughing
Laughing so hard
Laughing without reason
A laugh that has never come till now

I see intensity
I see willingness
I see me fearless
I see me hateless
I see me bowing
Bowing down to every single source of life
I see it all - ultimate liberation

Desperate aspirations

Teenage and heavy bags on shoulders
Desperate aspiration holders

Building blocks from rage to responsibility
Study and knowledge are not enough
Wisdom and ease are a must

Sitting in the classroom with dreamy eyes
With the dominant social media takeover
From spectrums of visions to bombastic decisions
Rhetoric cogitations to conquer destiny
Suppressed by parental pressure
Because they only can see engineers and doctors
Rest is inane to go for

Suicidal attempts budged from studies to Blue Whale, PUBG, Tik Tok
Failure of teenage love still prevails

Volitions for sex and drugs disguised into modern ways of living

Nevertheless, there is always a way out

Determination, understanding, the flaws of so-called unworthy reality

Dance along to the music of your inner voice

Which has guided you over ages to make the right choice

Raise your spirits high up,

To the tuning of what is sensible

It's about the journey and not destinations

There is always a subtle way to go for your desperate aspirations

Raindrops

Peeping out of my balcony's door,
I saw rain, trying hard to come in
Raindrops hanging to the grill
Shining like pearls falling down
I got a little pearl on my index finger
Didn't remain for long
Maybe my perception about life has been wrong

There's more happiness than sorrow
Sometimes you earn it, sometimes you borrow.

I then tried to catch another one
But it also went to dance with its pal
Raindrops are sometimes like best friends
Fall on earth, dance together, flow together
It's a virtue, still I pity
I pity on gravity that everything has to come down
Maybe that's the secret to rise

Improving your inner self making you wise
I tried for the third time
The drop remained for long this time
Kissed my finger hugged it and I let it go
Problems in life too are like raindrops
Hold them or let them go
decisions are up to you how you sow

Process

On the spot up and down
On the spot cheerful and with a frown
Together mixing up of feelings
Together with hard mind those dealings

With pleasure embracing of virtues
With debacle worries of future
How to handle when cluster of thoughts come
Never ending reasons in solitude
Have to showcase some firm attitude

Again a squally at the same time
Again so slowly at the same time
Will this be remembered or forgotten
Wanna leave all behind and start a new pattern
Dismiss all opinions and just live for this moment
Says the heart and soul that it should be your patent

Buoyancy is going far away
But can come here always to stay
Coming back to fantasies deep, dark and brown
On the spot up and down
On the spot cheerful and with a frown

A beautiful beauty

Coming through the bliss of a foggy morning
Waking up at the window, yawning
She's a blessed one, but it's only that
Doesn't carry a load of wholesome beauty pack
Though sweet voice, yet stubborn
Emphasizing on the dew drops on the leaves,
When she walks by the grass.

When she leaves I feel blue
When she turns around and see it's always new
The curvy edits in her body supersede autumns with springs

Oneiric gaze while an eye contact
Your clothes are making it distract
This tender nature needs assiduous attention
Smiling eyes peeping my soul are adorning
As I see you coming through the bliss of a foggy morning...

Welcome to
adulthood

Here you have to hide your actual true emotions and do not show them to people

Where you have to only smile when you feel like laughing

Where relations are nothing more than a formality

Where you have to show sympathy when you are actually happy because of someone's failure

Where you have to like the person you completely hate

Where you have to reject someone's demands because he didn't help you in trouble

Where you have to blindly follow the path everyone's following

Where you are not allowed to ask silly questions when u r actually confused

Where you have sit properly when you feel like to rest

Where you have to nod even if things are unknown to you

Where you have to gossip even when your conscience doesn't allow you to do so

Where you have to completely ignore even if someone's right and prove that you are always right

Where you have to always fight, fight and fight

Fight for money

Fight for fame

Fight for status

Where you have to eat with a fork and a spoon when u want to you're your hands

Where reality is more important than imagination

Adulthood is often confused with maturity

Whereas maturity is celebration of silence

Its forgiving the unknown

That's the real trouble with the world!

Too many people grow up before they are old

This is adulthood

Where you are not a child anymore

Where you have to behave as if you are the strongest, egoistic and the person with the correct attitude

My worst, best
friend

Once upon a time there was a princess,
unlike any other princess in my life

And we talked and talked for days and nights
She was crazy and didn't let me embrace her
We played until we were exhausted
And then she left...

We met again and she was more beautiful than before
We played until we were exhausted
Just like any other girl I too wanted to dress up like her

But I felt sad that I have to go away from her
There were just common occurrences of meeting her

I was glad whenever I would see her
There were laughters, there were jokes, there was bitching and too many eye candies

It was too wonderful in her world

I was still glad whenever I got to see her

Then she left again and I grew up to let go of her but I was sad....

and one day

bang she was in my life with clusterss of happiness joy and with an era that will last forever because time can surely set us apart but destiny cannot

We came close and no one was there to set us apart.

It was our time

It's as simple

When you'll see her you would want to be like her

Precisely a heart warming princess to just watch and when u know her more u wanna probe her more

Wanna be
nomadic!!

Why can't I just stay somewhere at night
As I am a night person
I like to sleep when I see dawn
Party high till 6 and then let a deep yawn

Why can't I just go anywhere I want
As I wanna enjoy the early mornings breeze
My night is only something I want to flaunt

We become night bee and just buzz around
We be the night butterfly and just smell the scent around

There should be no work there should be no load
For some exchange offers from the hippies and a long foggy road

We become easy birds and only fly high
We be the haunting one say the world good bye

There should be only friends and close friends
There should be only rains and a car so we can maintain the trends
Ours should be an absolutely sweet world
We blush, we tease, we stay happy; no mask
No fake hellos, no untrue help and no amenity
Days turning nights to days again and our road trip faciality

We be the bikers and go someplace high
There should be only solutions and no why
We be the roadies and we taste heavens highlighted

There should be wings to those dreams
That are not practical but just simple
Dreams that are clouded and candy flossed
Dreams which are shiny, bright and glossed

O dear God just a while I want
Where there are no tears and social idiotic pain
Where there is only to be what I want to be
And that is the want to be free

I want to walk around in the dark with you till morning
Where nightmare is a phrase (it's boring)
I want to sip the very first coffee of morning

We be the tasters of desserts
We be versatile in search of anything to make our taste buds happy
There should be all to say "we don't know...just keep going"

I want to just go away and create a new me; we, us and the skies
Where there are no worldly lies
Where I only need to follow where my heart leads

Where I dance with my soul crew
There should be some light music and some heavy snow
There should be beach and dolphins in a row
There should be jungle; there should be a sweet smell of trees
We should be always ready for excitement and its keys

I want to be blessed in the way
That when someone asks “feeling homesick”?
I say, “no way”!

Dear sadhguru!!

The ones living in the dark world
You,
Tempting your life to create peace within

I am in front of a player of words
And I need to be conscious enough to write
A piece of paper though cannot explain you
But your grace upon me will
I don't know whether I am forgetting you or living you some more
Your presence in everyone's lives is what I adore
Flowers of energies flaunt when around you
Like a small infant you too absorb everything around you
With you a bike ride in my mind is still due

What to say now!

Behold! We have a master of mystery
I won't let you be history
But a geography to the seeking ones
I am not thankful because
Thank you is just a small word
In front of what you've given to the world
A world which will be full of glee
Because you'll make it happen

My Guru!
Your practices welcome monsoons in my body
And make me a nobody
Nobody to all the dualities
Nothing good nothing bad
Nothing happy nothing sad
Just to the core glad
That you are!!
Yes you are!!
Inside me outside me I feel

Your chants appeal
To those lost
Somewhere between who am I
And to be or not to be

You know me more than I do
And
I don't know you more and more because of shambhavi
..
I can never get enough of you
Dear sadhguru!!
May you get the title of the only wonder in the world
What should I give you in front of what you have given me
Please do not forget me!
I am your humble servant
Bless me to see the unknown
And remind me that I am not alone!!

Beyond the magic

Beyond the magic of life there's faith
Faith to hold just one more last time
The creator's team is walking through your universe
Soul same colors are diverse
The eyes that see everything with passion
Count your blessings, make that a fashion
Adapt the strategy of being unknown to everything
Opportunities to explore
Will definitely explode
'Coz beyond the magic of life there's faith
'Cozy powers of relations that are worth...
Yes, not true but worth
Worth your expenses of sorrow and tears in pain
They may be friends or parents
The impetus they built, is a triumph

Between the earth and the sky
There are floating fantasies vs fractured souls
Who survive who fight
Who gives the path a light

Between boundaries and limits
There are energies that ask for liberty
A liberty which is within when born
The absence of white is black
There is duality in minds too

But this is the adventure that gives us power
Power to live
Power to soak the vibrations
That comes from the wind
Who gives us the signs
Signs to go beyond
Beyond the duality
Of light and dark

Good and bad
And become a despot
Of our own identity

Cheer up lady!!

Cheer up lady
Dance to the beat of life
It's Meera embodied inside of you
The source of power is Mother Earth
You are a proud maid and a queen at the same time
The odor of your soul is sublime
Being a being that has a womb to create men
Empowerment is just a base that you hold
Holding to rhythm of life you move
Move and show ways to the destiny
A compliment to the existence
A supplement to your surroundings
Wonderful one is you

Behold to the princess
Who is as pure as a driven snow
Every day is your day
Every hour is your hour

Every minute is your minute
Every second is your second
Cheer up lady
Dance to the beat of life
You are the Shakti,
You are the Shiva
You are the beauty alive

Either/or

Healthy relationships v/s empty emotions
Committed heart v/s self love verdict
Indeed friendship v/s solitude
Threshold discussions v/s limitless talks
A need for the mountains v/s a need for the sea
A relish for rains v/s citylights and unfree
A rapid shift from a we to me
Since birth there is always a need to be
Be yourself that is free
No reason and still a face full of glee
Escapism but with dignity
Head risen up like a grown up tree

Shadow

I don't know whether it's true or not
but I believe I love you a lot
Feeling every line of boundaries between us
We can't go a long way- not a matter to discuss
Those precautions of mind, that ignorance of heart
Will we be together or stay apart
Decisions are though strong yet fluctuate
Why these distances when we try to communicate?
I had sleepless nights
We had countless fights
We commented on each other I insulted you
We slept showing our backs to each other still you love me
Sometimes your presence is relaxing
Sometimes your absence is absurd
Let's pamper our dealings like a soul of a free bird

Everything's faded when we don't talk
Then I remember the time when we had a cozy walk
Those exaggerations in my mind when you touch me
The vibrations in my body when you feel me
The protective shield you build when you kiss me
Perhaps these scrums are necessary
A week or a month, they must remain temporary
Can I see you without me?
Can you see me without you?
If the answer is no,
Why wasn't it sorted a long time ago?
Commitments, priorities, words, expressions of sympathy
I think I lost you
Nobody to care, nobody to share, it was always you
Why do I think I lost you?

The long walk hands in hand
Our lovely footprints in the sand
Is this a small happiness or something grand?
How can I answer this?

How can you answer this anyway?
May this relation always go on with the shadow of milkyway

The dead tree

I saw a tree dead lying down at the side of a road
For some vivacious bird someday it was an abode
Many hold ups witnessed
Many accidents encountered

Making thousands of leaves orphaned
Penitence and dispraise to the entire fund
We are a part of them too
Making woods cry
Unseen are its tears
We cut and it bears

What karma has it gathered
Just lying down on the road side
Neither making shelter nor matchstick
If this soul is cut down for nothing
What would we suffer?

The tree never chooses a wrong path
Still doesn't receive the holy bath
A food for termites
Then turning into dust mites
A source of worship
Suffering countless hardships

The roots that were holding hands
Are now diverse not by choice
The one that is lifeless
Used to give life and rejoice
Have you ever hugged a tree,
And felt what it felt?
Millions of arrogant creatures
Still every heartful vision will melt

I saw a tree lying dead at the side of a road
Dead is not the tree
Dead is the community

Showing up a two day pity
Then enjoying their morning tea

Echoes of praises

Here I am sitting in front of the echoes of your praises
The emptiness that rarely one gets
But everyone chases
The birds, the walls, the trees, the nectar
That attest you here in this moment
They are a wholesome bliss of this bless
That enshrines within them
Throbbing hearts filthy minds
True devotees pure souls
Continuous interrogating
Ecstatic ones ignorant ones
Steady reasoning
One in all, all in one, come to see you
They experience happiness that is only given by you
They bestow to your very presence
Even in absence there is your presence
The very earth beneath you
The very sky above you

Listen to the hymns of your truth explained

The peaceful one, the blissfull one, the graceful ones are the undercovers that are fully trained

Tears

My tears are honestly mine
When eyes are satisfied, they are fine
True companions come out easily
When I am sad, happy or ecstatic

Looking up at the sky
I wanted to become clouds
They too cry when they are full
Full of life carrying within them
The tears they shower makes the earth feel shy
A unique love story with these elements
Earth and sky

Immediately pouring out when someone is born
At the moment pouring out when your loved one is gone

You feel and they fill, don't even ask
But concrete people deny them and wear a mask

Precious pearls kiss our cheeks and go
Although they are salty, they are still sweet when they flow

They are faithful therefore true companions
Washing your face and filling again
When I laugh too hard, they unconditionally remain

Love growth

Days are turning into glory
Since love bud became a flower
You have started coming into my imaginations now
Faults going unnoticed
About to be in love yet again
Nowadays tears are what I drain
Fruit of faith is strong currently
Laughing silly when eyes bang
Let it go through the waves
'Coz I wanna fall now
Fall for the happiness
Fall for the cuddle
Fall for the newness
The sensations to explore now
Won't let that go anyhow
Hold my hands in crowd
Hold it when passing by
Hold me from behind

But please be gentle and kind
Welcome monsoons in my body
Always, never ever say good bye
When it will go down, I'll definitely try
Superb are oceanic eyes
Still creating butterflies
Something's exclusive a brand new stock
Its madness when u talk
Had this been before
I would have never taken care of now
The one which was always taken for granted
Never knew it was always wanted
Staring at me makes me more beautiful
Obviously past was mischievous
And the fact was still unknown
The vacancy between strangers and best friends is filling soon
Whatever it is, it is a boon

Shenanigans
(fragrances of old age)

Deposited shenanigans
In the life's bank account

To tell stories
Collected everyday
And a new one each time

For my grandchildren
Sitting and sipping coffees
At the rocking chair
Beside the retro piano

In a room with fragrances of
Old age

Joys of destruction

Exit Pathways
That lead you to discouragement
But with dignity
That's what will guide you,

To the joys of destruction
That's when you will come out clean
To reveal the lotus
Out of the soiled environment

Passions crushed by living mates
The real life villains
Monsters with small egos
Fractured souls with haughty values

Faking your support and favour
Claiming that without them nobody is your saviour
Blindfolded pride easily piqued ones
Counting of them in every family

In abundance
They won't let you succeed
They know they are weak
They don't let you be happy
They know they are sad

Don't hand over your happiness to them
Unless you are a slave
Guess what? Times have changed
We are now absolutely brave

Your life is only your authority
Exit the Pathways that lead you to discouragement
But with dignity

Realization

The day you were born it was all messy and confused

But the day I realised the day you were born it was perfect

First time ever I thought of my perfect past

Your twinkling brown eyes

The purity within your cries

The compromises were now becoming compulsory

So was every moment that satisfied me

I was waiting for ages for this lifetime of a bliss

Never thought that my destiny would give a result like this

For that every cry of yours when your bed was wet

For that every temperature of yours feeling cold or sweat

Your smiling eyes, blushing cheeks, your perfect lashes,
Your itsy-bitsy hands
Always folded
When tried to open
The strong grip you had
In your hands my finger holding

The aroma of yours when I hugged you
The breath of yours when you were sleeping and I heard you
The laughter of yours when I hide it my face and surprised you
The cry of yours when you didn't find me next to you

Sitting next to me watching me dressing up, doing makeup
And copying my style
And I was only bursting upon you for that while

You were still craving
For my arms to sleep in
This paradise of your love was extremely deep
Time has passed but still you will be that tiny mine
When you came and cheered me up
When I was not at all feeling fine

A friend, a guide, a relation that can never be explained
You will have to go
With your prince one day
With your happiness gained

Maybe this is a reward
Of the blessing I received
In my past
Your love for me
And my love for you
Will always be very vast

May you be the best girl, sister, friend and mother

And best woman for your true soulmate

Yes! we're crazy

Mountains, Eternal, Sky High
Alcohol? What is it?
Our friendship. Wanna try?
Yes. We were strangers
Madness brought us together
Fun is what we are always ready to gather

The one who is serious get out
The one who is looney, welcome
No laws, no rules, just complete craziness
Honesty, simplicity, and of course dirty jokes and mess

Laugh out loud moments
Emotions are also present
Seriousness? That's always absent
The height of dreams we let fly high
The spirits will never die
To the melancholy it's our goodbye

Weird pictures, beer and skittles
Full high and glitters
Totally extended enjoyment
His fart and his embarrassment
Her demands to pee
Who's gonna drive next?
You, not me

The journey of life is insane
Like a felicitous view of a mountain
Like, the views outside
The window of a train

It's so beautiful
It's so wonderful
It's so lively let's relive
Inevitably an ocean of glee
Now it's not YOU, it's not ME, it's WE
In this world behold to see

See more madness around
To cheer, to cherish, to flaunt

This moment is the only truth present to be there, to love, to praise
Never to wait for something
Good to happen
Come all the weirdos
Come all the open-hearted ones
Come all the high-spirited ones
It's our welcome
This package is yet priceless
It's friendship in wholesome

Self-reverence

The tumults coming through and going down
Feelings that make you real but sometimes a clown,
True is the fact that you can never make anyone realize
The inner truth within the skies of your eyes,
That float in your mind always
That wanders inside and conveys
Those interactions with a closed one
Then interacting with your personal one

The bribe you give to yourself
Not to reveal
After getting caught the pity you feel
To be close to someone
Is that a punishment of virtue?
To have someone in your dreams
Pressurized by your mind why can't it be true?

Gracious simple moments to spend
Then praying that it should never end
Wonder if sentiments had a level
Simple, medium, expert
The world would then become a bunch of dirt
Some people are still available
Keeping a reputation of expert level

Your mind would then become a stock market
People will then carry them sadly in their heart's basket
I guess it's a matter of deeds
If expert level than humans
If the level is simple then you we'll be counted as a breed

I'm...yet to

I'm yet to
Pass through the gloomy vows of yours
Where we both were pretending to be happy

As betrayal was former
So was verbal violence

I'm yet to
Decide the rights and wrongs
As for you I was a dummy
The concealing of my bruises
That time was all crummy

I'm yet to burn those letters
Beside which you tried to burn my desires
How much do you love me when I asked
You were volunteering in the community of liars
I'm yet to live, that I will I know
As...
My love for you from that day expires

Beauty with the
beast

Her destiny is set to be free
Hopping from here to there
Like a crazy ball
No strong relations at all
Except the one (mother)
If she is in future

Very delicate by heart
No upsurge of mind
She's created in this way
If she smiles at happiness
Her illusion is defined as a slut

The weather in her body
Flows by all true emotions with the blood
Passing through all those feelings
She never gonna tell anyone
She still likes her past

The beast is sometimes her present
Her agreement with the pressure made upon her
Survival is her best policy in anyway
Get out get out get out
She screams loudly
Very loudly

Since birth despite of worldly revolutions
There's a demand of concession in every step
Strong enough to hold on her shoulders
Nobody can ever define that depth

Oh yes she's a baby when she's with the one
Oh no, no, don't assume wrong when she's alone
A needful of heavenly love is only the requisition
If yes standing strongly with pride will be her position

Come along she's a vending machine
Excreting tissue paper(expressions)
Use and throw
Reward for them who use it is a slap of truth

Stay strong, stay strong-her favourite line
Acceptation, pity , lust, certainly not the way to handle
She is a bud, a blooming flower
Still rotten up with mud she is

BEAUTY WITH THE BEAST

Afflatus is poetry

When I cover me by you,
You are like moreen
Gifting me with
Silences so serene

The wounds are healing
Without any substance
Eyes feel intoxicated
The ocean of words walks by my steps

The affinity between poetry and me
Is soulfully dedicated

This addiction to write
Is my supreme love

It's always inside nothing above
If I combine my quotes
And they start to rhyme

Would that be a boon or a crime?
Thoughts in my mind
Don't let me sleep
Afflatus is poetry beautiful and steep